MILITARY SHIPS
FRIGATES
BY JOHN HAMILTON

VISIT US AT
WWW.ABDOPUBLISHING.COM

Published by ABDO Publishing Company, PO Box 398166, Minneapolis, MN 55439.
Copyright ©2013 by Abdo Consulting Group, Inc. International copyrights reserved in all countries. No part of this book may be reproduced in any form without written permission from the publisher. A&D Xtreme™ is a trademark and logo of ABDO Publishing Company.

Printed in the United States of America, North Mankato, Minnesota.
042012
092012

PRINTED ON RECYCLED PAPER

Editor: Sue Hamilton
Graphic Design: Sue Hamilton
Cover Design: John Hamilton
Cover Photo: United States Navy
Interior Photos: All photos United States Navy except United States Naval Historical Center-page 12 insert (USS *Cuyama* with 12 frigates).

ABDO Booklinks
Web sites about Military Ships are featured on our Book Links pages. These links are routinely monitored and updated to provide the most current information available.
Web site: www.abdopublishing.com

Library of Congress Cataloging-in-Publication Data

Hamilton, John, 1959-
  Frigates / John Hamilton.
      p. cm. -- (Military ships)
  Includes index.
  Audience: Ages 8-15.
  ISBN 978-1-61783-523-0
  1. Frigates--United States--Juvenile literature. I. Title.
  V826.3.H36 2012
   623.825--dc23
                            2012005067

TABLE OF CONTENTS

FRIGATES

Modern frigates are small United States Navy warships. They are not as powerful as cruisers or destroyers.

The USS Crommelin *sails out of its home port in Hawaii.*

Perry-class frigates are named after American naval officers and other heroes.

Frigates are fast, tough, and relatively inexpensive. They are excellent armed escorts that protect other ships.

37

PERRY-CLASS FRIGATES

The United States Navy today has 26 frigates in its fleet. They are all Oliver Hazard Perry-class ships. Their hulls are long and narrow. The USS *Oliver Hazard Perry* was the lead ship in the class. It first sailed in 1977. Since then, many other Perry-class ships have been built.

XTREME FACT

Many older frigates, including the original USS Oliver Hazard Perry, *have been decommissioned and scrapped.*

The newest frigates were built in the late 1980s. Many frigates once carried guided missiles to protect against enemy aircraft. Today that ability has been reduced.

The USS Oliver Hazard Perry *(FFG-7), USS* Antrim *(FFG-20), and USS* Jack Williams *(FFG-24) sail together in 1982.*

MISSIONS

Oliver Hazard Perry-class frigates escort and protect other ships. They travel with amphibious assault forces and merchant convoys. Their main mission is anti-submarine warfare (ASW). Frigates have a limited ability to attack surface ships and enemy land targets. Frigates also stop ships that carry drugs and other illegal cargo.

Visit, board, search, and seizure (VBSS) team members from the frigate USS John L. Hall practice taking control of a vessel.

A visit, board, search, and seizure team from the frigate USS Elrod approaches a boat in international waters to check for illegal cargo.

HISTORY

For many centuries in the past, warships used sails. Frigates were ships that were fast and could turn quickly. They were wooden hulled. They usually had square-rigging on three masts.

The restored USS Constitution is the world's oldest commissioned naval vessel. It is open to visitors year-round at its home port of Boston, Massachusetts.

The USS Constitution sails by the frigate USS Carr in Boston Harbor in 2011.

Frigates weren't as heavily armed as large ships-of-the-line, but they were much faster. They often escorted other ships. They also patrolled coastlines and shipping lanes. The USS *Constitution* is the most famous U.S. Navy frigate. It was launched in 1797. It won many battles against British ships in the War of 1812. It earned the nickname "Old Ironsides."

The fuel tanker USS Guyama (center) sits surrounded by twelve Navy frigates in the early 1920s.

Starting in the 20th century, frigates were built with iron or aluminum hulls and used powerful engines instead of sails.

The frigate USS Brumby during a training mission in 1983.

Frigates were used to hunt submarines during World War II. During the Cold War, they were armed with long-range guided missiles. Today, those long-range missiles are no longer used. Frigates instead are used to fight submarines and close-range surface ships.

FRIGATES FAST FACTS

Oliver Hazard Perry-Class Specifications

Length:	453 feet (138 m)
Width (beam):	45 feet (13.7 m)
Displacement (loaded):	4,592 tons (4,166 metric tons)
Propulsion:	Two gas turbine engines, one propeller shaft
Speed:	29-plus knots (33.4 mph/53.7 kph)
Crew:	17 — Officers
	198 — Enlisted

The Oliver Hazard Perry-class frigate USS Elrod visits the naval station at Guantanamo Bay, Cuba.

ENGINES

Oliver Hazard Perry-class frigates are powered by two gas turbine engines. They are General Electric LM2500 engines. Both engines turn a single propeller shaft. Powered by these engines, frigates can cruise at speeds of more than 29 knots (33.4 mph/53.7 kph).

Perry-class engines are similar to the powerful engines used in DC-10 aircraft.

A technician checks the blades on a gas turbine engine aboard the frigate USS George Phillip.

TOUGH SHIPS

Oliver Hazard Perry-class frigates are small and inexpensive, but they are tough ships. In 1987, the USS *Stark* was struck and set ablaze by two Exocet missiles fired by an Iraqi jet in the Persian Gulf. Thirty-seven sailors were killed. The remaining crew put out the fire and sailed the *Stark* to port. Despite severe damage, the ship was eventually repaired and returned to duty.

The USS Stark *lists on its side after being struck by Iraqi-launched Exocet missiles in 1987.*

In 1988, the USS *Samuel B. Roberts* struck an Iranian mine in the Persian Gulf. No lives were lost, but the explosion blew a 15-foot (4.6-m) hole in the hull and flooded the engine room. Like the *Stark*, the *Roberts* was successfully repaired.

The cracked deck of the Roberts.

The damaged main engine room of the Roberts.

In 1988, the damaged USS Samuel B. Roberts is given a lift back to the United States, where it is fully repaired.

PHALANX CIWS

Perry-class frigates can defend themselves against enemy aircraft or missiles. When these threats get too close, the Phalanx CIWS (Close-In Weapon System) springs to life.

The Phalanx CIWS is fired during a training exercise aboard the frigate USS Boone.

The Phalanx CIWS is a rapid-fire gun that automatically tracks targets. It has a range of about 2.2 miles (3.5 km). Its Vulcan Gatling gun can shoot 75 tungsten armor-piercing rounds per second.

MK 38 CHAIN GUN

Some Perry-class frigates are fitted with the Mk 38 MOD 2 25mm (1 inch) chain gun system. The gun provides close-range protection against small enemy ships or floating mines. The Mk 38 MOD 2 can be remotely operated. Sailors can aim and fire the Mk 38 from the safety of the bridge.

XTREME FACT

The Mk 38 MOD 2 system has an effective range of about 1.8 miles (2.9 km). It can fire up to 180 rounds per minute.

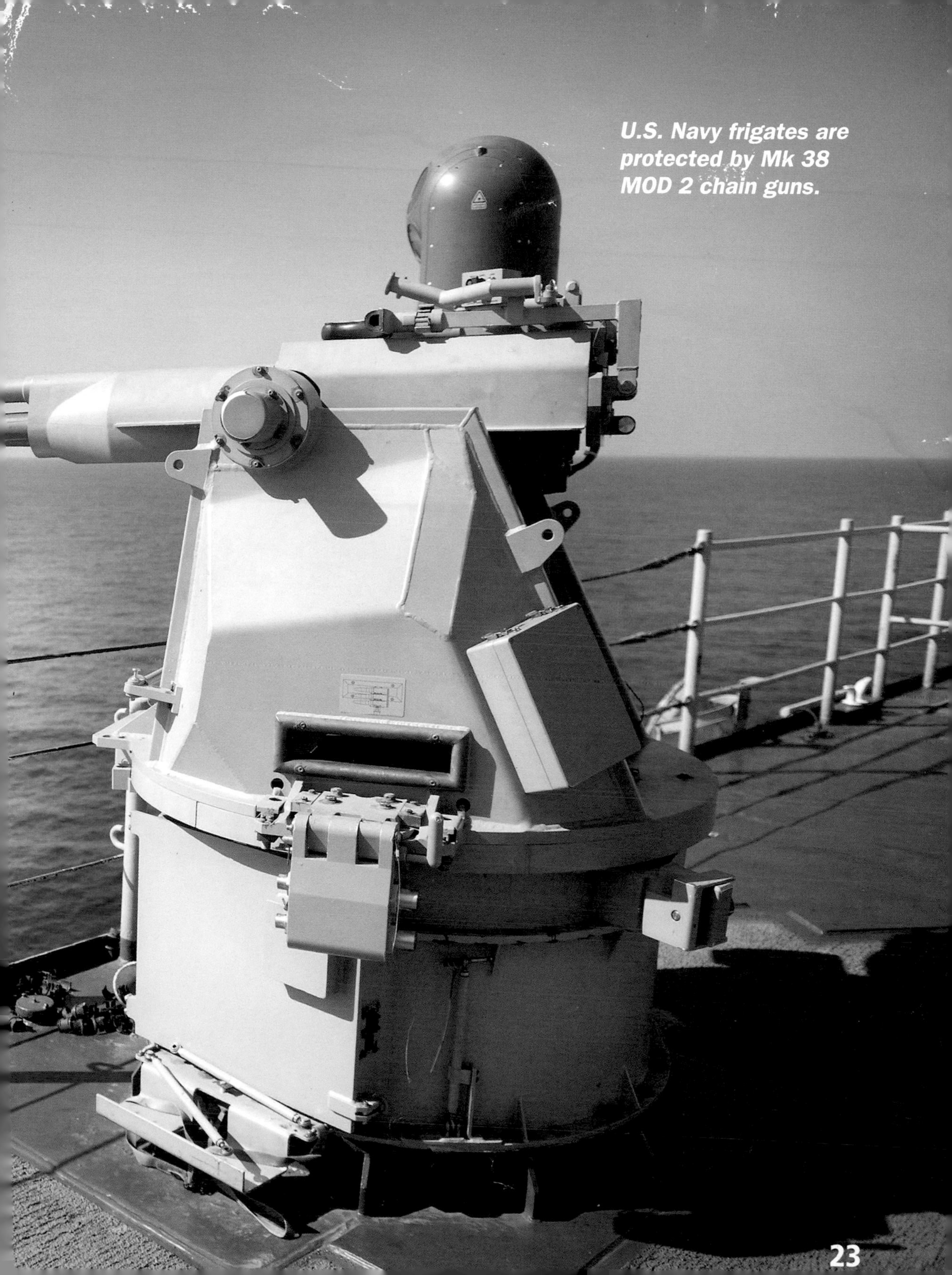

U.S. Navy frigates are protected by Mk 38 MOD 2 chain guns.

MK 75 GUN

U.S. Navy Perry-class frigates are armed with one large gun. It is called the Mk 75. It is a 76mm (3 inch) rapid-fire cannon made by OTO Melara and BAE Systems. It has a range of about 11.5 miles (18.5 km). It can fire 80 rounds per minute. The Mk 75 can be used against enemy ships and land targets. Because of its rapid-fire ability, it can even shoot down aircraft or missiles.

The Mk 75 rapid-fire cannon is fired aboard the USS Thach.

ANTI-SUBMARINE WARFARE

An important mission of U.S. Navy frigates is to protect the fleet from enemy submarines or mines. Perry-class frigates can trail a long sonar array behind them. It detects underwater objects. In addition, each frigate can carry two SH-60 Seahawk LAMPS Mk III helicopters. These helicopters use sophisticated sonar and electronics to detect submarines. They can also drop Mk 46 torpedoes to destroy enemy subs.

The USS Stephen W. Groves sails beside a South African navy submarine during a training exercise.

A Seahawk helicopter lands on the flight deck of the USS McClusky.

XTREME FACT

Some Seahawk helicopters can fire AGM-114 Hellfire missiles to protect frigates from enemy ships or targets on shore.

THE FUTURE

In the coming years, Perry-class frigates will be replaced by the Littoral Combat Ship (LCS). LCSs are small ships, like frigates. But they are armed with state-of-the-art weapons, as well as helicopters.

The USS Freedom *sails in the Pacific Ocean near Pearl Harbor, Hawaii.*

The Navy's first LCS ships include the USS *Freedom* and USS *Independence*. The *Independence* is a trimaran. It has three hull bottoms that are parallel to each other. It is a fast ship. It can travel at speeds up to 44 knots (51 mph/81 kph).

XTREME FACT

The "littoral zone" is the area close to shore. Littoral Combat Ships will fight other ships as well as ground forces along enemy shores.

The USS Independence *docks in Key West, Florida.*

GLOSSARY

COLD WAR
The Cold War was a time of political, economic, and cultural tension between the United States and its allies and the Soviet Union and other Communist nations. It lasted from about 1947, just after the end of World War II, until the early 1990s, when the Soviet Union collapsed and Communism was no longer a major threat to the United States.

DISPLACEMENT
Displacement is a way of measuring a ship's mass, or size. It equals the weight of the water a ship displaces, or occupies, while floating. Think of a bathtub filled to the rim with water. A toy boat placed in the tub would cause water to spill over the sides. The weight of that water equals the weight of the boat.

ENLISTED
A military service person who joined the armed forces, but is not an officer.

HULL
The hull is the main body of a ship, including the bottom, sides, and deck.

Radar

A way to detect objects, such as aircraft or ships, using electromagnetic (radio) waves. Radar waves are sent out by large dishes, or antennas, and then strike an object. The radar dish then detects the reflected wave, which can tell operators how big an object is, how fast it is moving, its altitude, and its direction.

Sonar

Technology that allows ships and submarines to detect objects underwater by measuring sound waves. An "active sonar" system sends out a burst of sound, a "ping" that travels through the water. When the sound wave hits an object, such as a ship or underwater obstacle, the wave is reflected back. By measuring the reflected wave, sonar operators can determine the object's size, distance, and heading. "Passive sonar" detects the natural vibrations of objects in water. It is most often used by submarines, because sending out an active sonar signal might give away the submarine's position.

World War II

A conflict across the world, lasting from 1939-1945. The United States entered the war after Japan's bombing of the American naval base at Pearl Harbor, in Oahu, Hawaii, on December 7, 1941.

INDEX